2 PORK CHOPS!

2 PORK CHOPS!

By John Masters

SOUND BOOKS PUBLISHING

This book is dedicated to Philip and Simone Burrows.
It is an honour and privilege to be your friend.
Your family are an inspiration.

ISBN 1 901044 01 7

Printed in Great Britain by
Caledonian International Book Manufacturing Co. Ltd.
Glasgow

For everyone who ever needs a miracle.

We live in difficult times, and in a world that offers little relief. Somebody once sung, *"Stop the world, I want to get off!"*.
Maybe we have all felt like that at times, but you can not just get off. Like little ants whose anthill has been crushed, we scurry around in circles, desperately searching for the answer, trying to make sense of it all.

Somewhere,
     Sometime,
          Somehow,
               everyone needs Someone

to come along and do the impossible or the incredible for them.

It may be trouble in the family, a financial crisis, a broken heart, or a messed up life. Perhaps it is shattered dreams, or a life-threatening illness. Or it may be the need of a job, a long-awaited answer, somebody to love you, or just finding a reason to go on;

but whatever it is, there is an answer - there is a miracle just waiting to happen - for you!

I've seen a few myself.

This book tells about some of them, but more importantly, it shows the secret for releasing that desperately needed miracle.

> *"To every thing there is a season,*
> *And a time to every purpose under heaven."*
> *(King Solomon)*

This is your time, your season,

if you can dare to believe!

Discovering a Miracle.

I sat alone on the edge of the sea, the moon bathing the stillness of the night with its mellow radiance. The gentle lapping of the waves against the rocks seemed to melt away the rush and tear and struggle of yet another day. How wonderful, how beautiful to be alive! And in some strange way, it felt really good to be alone!

I thought of the poem that I had learned as a small child,

"What is this life if full of care,
We have no time to stand, and stare?"

I needed this time to just stop; to take time off, or as they say, 'chill-out'. My greatest enemy was boredom (I hate being bored!), and so I filled my life with activities and projects, and worked as hard as I could to achieve results. However, every morning I would come down to this spot and walk along the coastal path to think and prepare for the day ahead, and just for a change, I ventured back down after work on this particular evening to get away from it all.

There were a hundred and one things pressing me for attention, and I could do with a few miracles to sort some of them out, but I just popped them all into a little drawer inside my mind, and decided to enjoy the air and freedom of the night.

And there it was!

Right in front of my eyes, staring down at me.

A marvel. A wonder. A miracle indeed!

That lonely, desolate planet, we call the moon, hung there in a cloudless sky, filling the entire 'nightmospherics' with a sense of hope and expectancy.

I say a marvel, a wonder, because truly that's what it is.

By all accounts, I am told, the moon is dead:

a cold and lifeless spectacle that at first sight has no apparent value, and no sensible reason for being there.

But every night by some peculiar chance of nature, a metamorphosis takes place. (I like that word. It means 'to change as if by magic'.)

This barren loneliness, trapped in time and space, is transformed from darkness into light.

That great light of our solar system, the sun, shares its power and glory with a nothing.

Meaningless finds purpose: this moon suddenly finds reason for being - a miracle indeed!
Surely no chance or accident this, but master-minded in a perfect plan.

I thought, "If there is a reason for the moon, then there is a purpose for my life as well."

Miracles come in all shapes and sizes.

To be precise, I suppose that a miracle might be the birth of a child, the supply of money, the curing of a dreadful illness, peace in time of trouble, or just finding a reason to go on.
It is not always the obvious though, and sometimes it is the most unlikely source that brings it about.
However, there is always a key to the miracle - but we have to discover what that key is.
The key that causes the moon to shine is its 'position'. Its position in relation to the sun brings about the miracle.

We may not like the key when we first discover it, but if the door to your miracle is ever to be opened, the lock must first be turned.
This book presents the key.

This book could be dangerous. It may just be your position that is preventing the miracle from happening.

It could change your life.

Looking for a miracle? Perhaps there's one just in front of your eyes!

Miracle at School.

A little about nothing really!

One of the earliest miracles that I encountered happened during my second year at grammar school.
I have always found it much more enjoyable to do practical things than to sit down and study. During the first year I managed to skip the best part of the first nine months of schooling by just not bothering to go. This was probably because I

had a brick thrown at my head during the first week there, and subsequently I would spend most days walking around London trying to find scrap metal to make some easy cash.

I had a friend called Pickles, (that was his surname actually), and together we used to get up to some mischief at times!

I don't think that we went to a single P.E. lesson for two and a half years after the sports master picked me up off the ground by my hair for not having training shoes (my parents could not afford any).

We found a wonderful old lady who lived in a bungalow just round the corner from the school. She used to make us a pot of tea and supply us with biscuits and cakes during P.E. lessons whilst all the other kids were busy exercising.

Rocket hits school!

One afternoon, school being ended, we drifted slowly and aimlessly through the corridors towards the main entrance. The cleaners had left a bucket and mop outside one of the classrooms and instinctively I grabbed the mop and ran round the corner. The anticipated shouting of an irate cleaner failed to materialise, so we slowed our run to a walk.

We heard some noises coming from another room where the door was half-open.
Inspiration flashed across my imagination. The mop suddenly 'transformed' into a rocket! The rocket was prepared for launch.

Countdown! Aim! Fire!

We have lift-off!

Flying mop hits teacher.

Teacher rendered unconscious!

We ran, but were not quick enough. Somebody spotted us.

Funnily enough, that same evening as I was making my way home from a friend's house, I slipped on the ice and ended up in hospital with concussion.

The teacher, who had been so unfortunate to be in the wrong place at the right time, was in fact my English tutor. She was a good teacher, and I enjoyed English more than any other subject.

When I went back to school a week or so later, I had to apologise to her, and then report to the headmaster's office. We called him 'Killer'!

He was some mean character, with sharp pointed features, a Hitler-type moustache, and dark beady eyes. When you saw him coming down the corridor you hid out of sight until he passed, if you were anything like me.

I was not his most popular pupil. In fact, on one occasion he ordered me not to stand outside the front of the school buildings because it would give the school a bad name!

Pretending to have a severe headache due to the concussion, I avoided six of the best that day. But this was to be only a temporary reprieve. My excuse began to wear thin after two weeks, and 'Killer' said it must be delayed no longer. The long, thin, bamboo cane came out of his desk. I leant across his two-armed chair, and my punishment was meted out. Six stinging strokes across one's rear end!

At the end of term, some little while after, I was handed, by my class tutor, an official-looking Report book. This large A4 black book was decorated in gold with the name of the school, and contained an indelible record of assessments and comments along with my results for exams and yearly achievements. This was a frightening day - my father would be waiting for this!

Imagine my absolute astonishment and surprise when, turning to my English teacher's comments, I found that she had given me an incredible A+ for my years work, and 99% for my exam results! There was no mention whatsoever of my misdemeanour.

This was the first miracle that I had ever seen.

OK, so maybe my teacher was just dead nice, but to me it was a miracle!

Back from the Dead!

Whilst living in the South West, I worked in a sawmill for three years, and during the evenings and weekends I would hitch a lift over to a little village called Chulmleigh.

There I had the great privilege of studying out in the country with my own personal tutor. Whilst everyone else went to college, I took advantage of the extraordinary opportunity to be privately taught in the comfort of a large rambling farmhouse.

As there were never any college fees to pay, and no charge placed on me for my tutor's time, I always considered it an honour to help around the estate whenever possible.

During the summer of 1980 the local farmer who was contracted to cut and bale the fields of hay got behind on his work-schedule. The grass had been cut, but he was quite unable to turn it ready for baling.

It was essential that the hay was brought in as soon as possible to keep it fit for the horses during the winter season.

I volunteered my services, and promised to get a tractor and hay-turner within the next couple of days. (The estate did not have its own machinery for the job.) Down in another village I managed to borrow a David Brown tractor from a local farmer (well, his son actually - the farmer was away on holiday), and located an old Cock-Pheasant turner at another farm.

The farmer showed me briefly what lever did what, and which switch turned this or that on, and, hoping that I would remember the essentials, I set off towards the road. I had never driven a tractor before, and used the twelve miles to the estate to get the hang of all the controls.

Over the next few days I was pretty successful in turning the hay, in spite of getting the machine entangled in the barbed-wire several times.

About a week later I received a telephone call from the farmer's son asking me to return the tractor as it was required for some work the next day. I caught the 5 a.m. train the following morning to Chulmleigh, and climbed up over the hills to where the tractor was. I knew that if I could get it back before 7 o'clock I would still be able to get to work on time at the sawmill.

As a child, I had been taught to say my prayers at the start of every day, and so it did not seem an odd thing for me to stand out there in the field and say, "Oh God, whatever happens today, let it be under your perfect control." That was to be a prayer that I would never ever forget!

I started up the engine and put the David Brown into gear. It was an older tractor and had no cab (which made me very grateful that it was not raining). I rattled along at a fair pace and decided to take a shortcut down a single-track lane to save going on the main road.

This lane suddenly turned into a 1 in 3 hill with two very sharp bends half way down. I was travelling in high gear as I approached the top of the extremely steep incline. I knew that I had to slow down because, even if I could negotiate the first corner, I would never get round the second one.

If I didn't slow down I would end up going over the edge of the road and crashing onto the other road some fifty feet below.

I reached for the gear-stick and depressed the clutch. The gear would not budge! Being an old tractor, there was no synchromesh in the gearbox - I had forgotten about that! I hit the brakes trying not to over-brake in case it went into a skid.

Nothing happened! The brakes had failed. I remember looking back to see if I was skidding on the grass verge perhaps, but no, those big rear wheels were still turning unabated.

I had a choice. It's funny how quickly the mind works when you find yourself in frightening situations. I could just jump off and let the tractor plunge to the road below, but what if there was another vehicle there? I remembered my father telling me as a child that if ever the brakes were to fail on the car, the best course of action would be to use the gears to slow you down, or try to edge the car into the bank on the side of the road.

I had already tried the first option. It didn't work! Half on, half off the tractor, I committed myself to trying to jam the tractor into the raised bank along the verge.

I remember the tractor beginning to climb.

On their way to work that morning, two men travelling in a van decided to take a shortcut up a very steep hill. On rounding the first corner they came across a tractor upside down in the middle of the road. It was still rocking to and fro. Jumping out, they realised that there was someone underneath the wreckage.

The rear wheel of the tractor was virtually bent in half, the huge engine had sheared off its mounting plates, and diesel was running from the tank down the hill.

One of them ran up the road to a farmhouse about four hundred yards away, from where they called the emergency services. Returning to the scene with a local farmer, they waited for the police and ambulance to arrive.

The nearest hospital was a good 18 miles away, but as far as any of them were concerned the young man underneath the tractor was dead.

Motionless, he lay there with his eyes wide open, staring up at the blue sky.

Eventually the police arrived, and, as they were looking on, the farmer saw what he said was just a little 'twitch' in the cheek of the young driver. "Thank God!" he cried, "he's alive! - get him out!"

Apparently, (though I was quite unaware), after they had pulled me free, I went quite berserk!
One of the chaps at the scene told me some weeks later, "We pulled you out OK, but then all hell broke loose! We could not hold you as you dragged two of the policemen down to the bottom of the hill. You were constantly smashing your head against the road, and I feared that you would kill yourself."
In fact this man eventually put his leg underneath my head to stop any further damage being sustained. As a result he had to bandage his leg, and went round with a walking-stick for some weeks after!

I was aware of a foreigner asking me what my name was. It sounded as though he was down a long tunnel, and it annoyed me that he kept asking the same question. I was sure that I had answered him the first time. There was a terrible pain in my head, and I was trying to figure out where I was. I thought that I was lying on the kitchen table at my old friend, the Colonel's house! This did not make a whole lot of sense, but then nothing did at that moment.

My parents had been rushed to the hospital with a police escort after being asked to identify a shoe belonging to me. They were told that I had sustained serious injuries to my head, and did not know what internal damage I might have. They were advised that I would have serious brain damage for the rest of my life. I did not recognise them and did not make any response to their questions as I lay in the intensive-care room.

It must have been midday when I actually came round. For the rest of the afternoon and night my body went through severe spasms every few minutes, all my muscles suddenly seizing, bringing my knees violently up into my chest. This quickly sapped me of the little strength that I felt I did have.

At three in the morning I asked the nurse for a drink, my throat being as dry as the desert. She eventually brought me a teaspoonful of water in the smallest beaker that I have ever seen. I felt insulted, and would not even touch it!

At seven a.m. I looked in the locker next to my bed, and found most of my clothes were there. I put on the diesel-soaked, blood-splattered T-shirt, and the torn trousers, but failing to find my shoes, walked barefoot out of the ward down to reception. I have always hated hospitals! There I called a taxi, and by 8 o'clock I was knocking on my parents' front door asking them to pay the cab driver. They were stunned, to say the least!

Not a bone in my body was broken, and within three weeks I was back at work.

The police came to see me and said, "You should be dead!"

I visited my doctor, who sat back in his chair just shaking his head in amazement. He said, "What are you doing here? You shouldn't be alive!"

I have no doubt whatsoever that my miraculous survival came as a result of that little prayer out in the field that morning.

Oh yes! I believe in miracles!

£62-29p Miracle.

I guess that I had always believed to some degree in God, but not to the point that it made any difference in my life. I remember the time that I was locked up in a police cell in Hastings at the age of eighteen for something rather stupid that I had done. They removed my belt and my shoelaces, in case I hung myself with them I suppose! Well, I prayed that day! I said, "God, if you get me out of this, I will be the best person that you have ever seen!"

In fact, when my case went to court, I was given twelve months' conditional discharge. I thought to myself, "Brilliant God! But look, I'll become a good Christian when I'm eighty years old. I want to live my life first, make some money, and have a good time." The trouble is, none of us have any guarantee on the length of our life.

It was actually just two years later that I did became a Christian. As a result my whole life was revolutionised, and my perspective altered. I discovered purpose and meaning to life, and I began to experience real miracles in my everyday circumstances. I share some of these experiences in the next pages, and I hope that one of them might strike a chord with you. Perhaps the miracle you require seems daft to everyone else, but to you it is of great importance. All things are possible to him or her who can believe!

Maybe, like the moon, you just seek a reason for being. But whatever the miracle, remember, the sun is always shining; the moon must simply come into position before it catches the light.

Somebody once said, "It is better to give than to receive". In our high speed, instant cash, instant credit, money grabbing society, this philosophy does not have much chance of being believed.

However, I became a believer in this principle around July of 1976, and I'll tell you why.
This is one of the little miracles that helped build my faith and confidence to expect even greater things.

There were not many things that I owned or possessed that I considered of any great value, but I did have a six-string EKO guitar which I could not very well do without.
This was not because I was a talented guitarist, (in fact I struggled to play anything unless it was in the key of C), but rather due to the children's work that I was involved with every weekend.
I used to go down to the park in East Ham (London) with a couple of 'real' musicians, and hold an outside get together for the local children.
We would do a few songs, tell a story (their favourite was about a man-eating plant), and get the kids involved in a bit of activity.

One of the guitarists (Mick) who worked with me, had recently come over from Australia where he had been touring with a band. He is an extremely talented blues and classical guitarist, but had got mixed up in the drug scene and subsequently had become a heroin addict.

It was while he was out in Aussie that a massive change occurred in his life, (as a direct result of reading the Bible), the effect being that he was completely set free from his addiction without going through any 'cold-turkey'!

When I first met him he weighed just 6 stone 6 ounces, and stood around six feet tall!

I was sitting in my bedroom one night and felt that perhaps I should give Mick my guitar as he himself did not have his own, and was constantly borrowing one. I struggled a bit over this and thought, "I need my guitar for the kids' programme, I'm out of work, not 'signing-on', and can not afford to buy another one; how can I give it away at this time?"

After an hour or so I gave in and made a decision to let Mick have it. God says that if you give, it will be given to you, and so I took Him at His word and gave my friend the guitar.

It was around two weeks later on the 25th February that I received a letter from the Inland Revenue. (It was my birthday funnily enough). Inside it was a cheque for £62-29, and I immediately knew that God had answered my prayer for another guitar.
You see, I had been praying to God and explaining to Him that I really did need another instrument so that I could carry on the children's work.

When the cheque came, I instinctively knew that this was the answer to my specific prayer.
I caught a bus to Ilford where there was a little music shop by the traffic lights. I walked in and looked all around at the dozens of different guitars available. What did I know about guitars?
My attention was drawn to one high up hanging from the ceiling. It was a beautiful sunburst colour with little humming birds on its belly and mother-of-pearl inlay all around its circumference.

The only drawback was that it had 12 strings instead of 6. It was hard enough for me to play on six strings with four fingers let alone twelve with the same, but I figured that if there were twice as many strings then the sound would be twice as good as well!

There was no price tag on the guitar and I asked the shop assistant to get it down for me.

Yes! - this was the one!

I asked him for a plastic carrying case, a plectrum, a capo, and a strap, to go along with it, and then asked him how much it all was. He totalled it up on a piece of paper and said, "That will be £62-29 please."

I said, "Would you take a tax-man's cheque?"

He said "Yes", and I went down the road a step higher up the ladder of faith!

Yes! You see, God is not *nearly* right, He's always, only ever, spot-on!!

This was a wonderful miracle to me in those early days as a new believer, and it would be so easy to dismiss it as just coincidence if it was not for the fact that these sort of 'coincidences' continued to happen and grow both in frequency and size!

I was to see and experience greater miracles than this.

Jed

Jed was just a few months old when we moved into our new home on the Island. He was a bright spark with a beautiful smile, and was adored by all who saw him. His birth was miraculous owing to the fact that he should have been born dead or brain damaged due to the shocking negligence of the maternity staff at the Hospital.

I had made myself a really decent mug of tea, piping hot, (the only way to drink it!), and placed it on top of the hearth next to the gas fire. It was a cold night, and I turned the fire up fully before picking up the baby and sitting down in front of the coal-effect, living-flame, artificial, but very effective heater.

You are told never to place hot liquids within reach of a baby or toddler. The information brochure for new parents warns of the dangers of hot substances to children. A cup of tea spilling over a baby is like pouring a boiling kettle over an adult.

Naturally I was always cautious of where I put my drink in case one of our other children accidentally spilled it on themselves, but for some unknown reason that night I had placed the drink down on the tiles just three inches above floor level. Perhaps I did not consider it a reason for concern with the baby only being a few months old and the other children in bed. I laid him down on the floor in front of me.

Things happen so quickly that you are not always quite sure how they came about. So it was this night. In a split second, what should have been a very relaxing half-hour, turned into every parent's nightmare!

Without me even noticing, Jed had somehow reached out and grabbed the mug, pouring the contents all over his chest and arms! His scream pierced the night, and brought my wife running from the other room.

There are certain distinctions in a child's scream that parents have a unique and intimate knowledge of. You know when they are hurting. There is the scream of anger, the cry for attention, even the 'pretend I'm hurt' cry, but there is something else in the cry of genuine pain and anguish, that, although quite undefinable, is quickly recognised by a mum or a dad.

Such was the scream this time. Immediately noticing what had happened, I grabbed Jed and cried "Oh God!". I did not mean it irreverently, but knew that He was the only one who could help me. I ran through to the kitchen with him and thrust him under the cold water tap.

He had one of those all-in-one grow-suits on, and I just immersed him in the water that filled the sink. His screaming increased as the cold water added to his discomfort, and I tried to calm him by talking to him. "It's all right, it's all right; I've got you, I've got you!"

I kept him submerged for some minutes before rushing him back into the living room. I put him down on the carpet and began to undo his clothing. His chest and left arm were bright red where the scalding tea had permeated his thin blue grow-suit. I noticed the skin beginning to rise into what I knew would be blisters.

The nearest hospital was over twenty five miles away and would take a good half-hour to drive to even if the road was clear. The ambulance would take even longer because it would have to come all the way across the Island first. I quickly wrapped a wet towel around him and just prayed over him. I said, "God, I pray against what I can see. Let these blisters go down right now. Heal this little body by Your power, in the Name of Jesus Christ!"

I held him and comforted him until he slept, and then placed him in his cot under the care of a God that I had come to trust and love.

Sometime later I picked him up from his cot, and placing him on the bed in the other room, I undid

his clothes. There were no blisters, and not so much as even a pink patch anywhere on him. God had heard my cry, and answered my prayer!
The Bible says, "Call unto me in the day of trouble, and I will hear you, and save you!"

I did, -
He did!

Scared to die!

A lady came up to me one evening at the end
of a young people's meeting with tears running
down her face.

She demanded to know who had been talking
to me about her! I told her that I did not even
know who she was, and that if something I
had said affected her in some way, then it was
not because I knew anything of her situation.
She said that everything that I said was to do
with things in her life! I suggested that perhaps
it was God trying to get through to her.

She went on to tell me that she was just 35 years old, but had only six months to live. She was dying of a virulent cancer. She said, "I'm so scared! - I'm scared to die!"

I told her that I would like to sympathise over her sickness, but would not at that time. She looked astonished!

I said, "Your sickness will undoubtedly bring you to an early grave, but there is something far worse that will bring your soul to a lost eternity, outside of heaven and all that is good."

Well she just looked at me!

I explained to her, that, like all the human race, she had a spiritual problem. There is a spiritual sickness inside all of us called 'sin' that bars us from God's presence, and ultimately, will send us to hell.

Well, she cried a whole lot more.

I was a bit amazed at myself afterwards when I came to consider what I had said, especially in the light of her terrible affliction.

I never heard from her again until she turned up at our Tuesday youth night two weeks later.

She was a different woman. There was a broad smile on her face, and a confident assurance in her eyes. She told me that when she got home that night after speaking with me, she considered what I had said. She decided that what she had heard that night was true, and asked God to forgive her sin, and accepted Jesus Christ as the answer to her life.

She told us that she had to put right some of the things in her life that she knew were wrong, and after praying to God, she felt clean and brand-new inside.

She was no longer afraid of death, and told me not to pray for her to be healed, because she wanted to go to meet this Jesus face to face!

Well, I tell you, that was a bigger miracle than if she had been healed right there on the spot!

The Bible tells us that Jesus came to destroy him who had the power of death (that is the devil), and set people free from its fear and terror.

She moved from her position of *'fear'*, and stepped into the position of *'faith'*.

2 Pork Chops!

You may have been one of those people fortunate enough to have been born into a rich family, although I think that that may not necessarily be the best way to be born.

I was not. We struggled through, and learnt to survive. I remember going to school with the soles of my shoes tied to their uppers with string!

When I was a child there were no designer label track shoes, or fancy named sweatshirts costing ridiculous prices. You wore what you were given, and tried to make it last as long as possible, especially when you grew up in a large family as I did. I had nine sisters and three brothers eventually!

Most of my shoes and clothes came from the jumble-sale, and it would never have entered my mind to ask my parents for anything more. We learnt that money did not grow on trees, and every penny really did count. As a result we appreciated the little things in life, and never more so than at Christmas.

The thrill of Christmas Eve has left an indelible memory of excitement, anticipation, and happiness, on my life. We would hang up our little socks at the end of our beds, and wait for my father to say good night to us.

About three hours later we would still be wide awake listening to the rustle of wrapping paper and general chit-chat between my Mum and Dad downstairs. Sometimes we would hear Santa's bells ringing, and around midnight Santa could be heard climbing the stairs! We all pretended to be asleep as his footsteps approached the bedroom. Peeping out from under the bedclothes we could just make out his red suit and white beard, but as quickly as he had come he vanished out of the room again.

We would jump up to see if there was anything in our socks, but alas, Santa had not done his job - they were still quite empty! It was oh, so difficult to get to sleep, and when eventually we did doze off, it was not for very long.

At 5 o'clock we were jumping up again to have another look at the foot of our beds, but still nothing there. We sneaked downstairs and into the living-room, and there, hanging over the fireplace, were not our short little socks, but several long grey socks filled to the brim with all sorts of goodies. Our parents never complained at their lack of sleep that night, but enjoyed all of the fun and excitement as we unpacked all that Santa had stuffed into those socks, spilling it onto their bed at that unearthly hour!

I guess we worked out pretty quickly that our Dad was Santa, but we enjoyed playing along with it, and it made no difference to our joy and happiness.

Christmas dinner was always the best, with the biggest turkey you have ever seen! Dad always carved, and our plates were just loaded to giant size. We would sing a grace (that really was the worst part!) and then tuck in and eat like kings.

We had to wait all day until the early evening before we went into the 'best room'. This was where the Christmas tree and our presents were displayed. We never got to see the tree or the decorations until it was dark on Christmas night. The room was locked, and the curtains drawn all day against prying eyes!

Before going into the room we all had to wear blindfolds as part of the preparation for what to us was the most important moment of the whole year. Once inside, the blindfolds were removed, and a tree covered in amazing lights in the shape of snowmen, Santa Clauses, and other Christmas characters met our widened eyes. Paper garlands seemed to cover the entire ceiling, and intriguing shaped presents cluttered the floor around the base of the Christmas tree.

It may have been second-hand, but my father had spent hours and hours cleaning and repainting that huge blue and red tipper truck that was hidden within the wrapping paper with my name tag on it. When I opened it, the thrill on my face was sufficient reward to my dad for all of his hard work. To me, it was the best gift in all the world.
Of all my childhood Christmas presents I remember the big lorry, and a wind-up metal submarine. It was a clockwork submersible that used to duck and dive in the bath every time you wound it up. I think that my father bought it for himself really, the time he spent playing with it in the bathroom! It rusted out in the end.

Little things in life are so important!

When I was about nine years old, I went to Dungeness lighthouse on a school outing. I have never forgotten opening my packed lunch to find, to my delight and suprise, a whole portion of cooked chicken in there. I felt very special and privileged that day! I had never had a shop-bought piece of roasted chicken to myself before.

I guess it must be hard for young people today, here in the West, to appreciate how valuable these early memories are. In all of our fashion-conscious, materialistic, disposable, easy-come-easy-go, society, such little things have no relevance.

"Give me, give me, give me!" is often the only language spoken by kids these days.

But it is the little things in life that are so important, and one's appreciation of such small incidents and gifts produces a quality of character that is so rare.

A funny Miracle!

In Great Britain they say that one person in every five hundred is a millionaire! I happen to take up residence among the four hundred and ninety nine that are not!

I often wonder what it would be like to win, say, five million pounds in the National Lottery. I do not think that I would like to. You see, I would miss out on all those wonderful little miracles that I would not need anymore, simply because I could 'afford it now'.

It has been those incredible 'in the nick of time' miracles that have given such quality and diversity to my life. You know, that time when a bill is shouting at you to be paid immediately, and you, being stony broke, cannot raise any cash. Out of the blue, someone comes round with the money they owed you from six months ago.

Or like the time that the Land Rover, (which we had borrowed), broke down just outside London. We were an awful long way from home with six or seven other people, and wondered how we would get back that night with no spare money available.

The temperature gauge had gone ballistic, and the maximum speed I could get from the engine, even downhill, was 30mph!

Thinking that I had lost all of the oil or something, I pulled on to the hard shoulder, and attempted to inspect the engine in the pitch black (it was around 1.30am). Not being able to see a thing, I decided to have another go at getting the vehicle home to Devon.

We did not get very far. I pulled over yet again, and had another look inside the engine compartment. It was no good, I couldn't see a thing, and even if I could have, there was very little that I could have done in any case.

Prayer changes things!

Whilst I was outside in the rain the guys in the back of the Land Rover decided that some prayer might help the situation. After all, if God made the heavens and the earth, and created the first man that ever lived, then was a turbo-deisel engine such a big problem to Him?

I jumped back in unaware that they had prayed about the situation, and put it into gear.

We travelled for the next three hours down the M3/A303 at 70mph with the temperature back to normal!

It doesn't finish there either!

On arriving in Barnstaple, I dropped off each member of my team, and finally arrived at my own house in the early hours. After parking up, I switched off the engine, and caught a few hours' sleep.

I decided that I would return the vehicle straightway to the garage and tell them of our difficulty the night before.

In the morning I went to turn the key in the ignition, but nothing happened. It was absolutely dead. There was not a spot of life in it. The garage had to come and transport the motor away. They informed me a week later that the problem was caused by the timing chain coming off! The whole engine would have to be rebuilt due to the 'rods' going up into the cylinder head. All four pistons and bearings would have to be replaced along with the cylinder head itself! They could not believe that we had driven that vehicle all the way from London after such a catastrophic breakdown.

Or like the time I needed £3,750 by Friday lunch-time, and like today is Thursday! I prayed and asked God, in the name of Jesus, to meet my need. On Friday, at lunch-time, two young men walked up my drive and knocked on the door. They said, "Today is a very special day for you!", and handed me a personal cheque for £3,750.

So, why '2 Pork Chops'?

Some years ago when we lived in Devon, we were really struggling to make ends meet. All that we seemed to do was to pay bills! As soon as one lot was cleared, another pile would arrive on the doorstep with the postman. I had no salary or income to speak of, and we were not drawing any government allowances because we were engaged in a full-time Christian ministry.

Every morning I would drive out a little into the country lanes to go for a walk. This was, and still is, the most important habit that I have ever formed. This is where I developed my friendship with God and came to know more of His Son Jesus Christ.

One particular morning in the summer, the sun was rising high in the beautiful blue sky, and I was enjoying the warm air and the freedom and peace of the countryside. The single track lane that had become one of my favourite haunts, was alive with flowers and shrubs. It was a wonderful place to think and talk things through with God.

As I was walking I noticed something in the hedgerow. Walking over to it, I was amazed to discover two dinners sat right inside the hedge, on separate trays, covered with cellophane. I prodded them and discovered that they were frozen solid.

On each tray there was chips, peas, and two pork chops!

Well, I just smiled to myself, and wondered how on earth they had got there. This little lane was hardly ever disturbed by traffic, and it was quite unusual to find anyone else down there. Here was something most bizarre! Now, I know that Moses came across a *'burning'* bush, but I came across a *'frozen-dinner'* bush!"

The hedge was quite a few feet off the road, which made it most unlikely that they could have fallen from a passing vehicle. I sort of frowned to myself in astonishment, and continued my walk.

On arriving home some time later, I told my wife that I had seen an incredible sight whilst out walking. I said, "You'll never guess what I saw today!" Well she never did.

So anyway, I told her, and she just said, "Why didn't you bring them home? That was God providing our dinner for today - we've got nothing else to eat in the house."

I said, "What? - You think so, huh?"

"Do you want me to go back and get them (if they're still there, of course)?"

"Yes!" she replied!

Well, I got back in the car somewhat bemused, and drove out to the lane. There they were, still sitting there, still frozen, still inside the hedge! I brought them home, and at lunch-time she duly cooked them.

Now, me being quite the sceptic, I watched her eat the meal waiting to see if she were to drop down or something, thinking them to be poisoned!

I said, "Is that good?" She replied, "Excellent!"

After a while, and seeing that she was still alive, I figured that perhaps this was God's extraordinary way of providing for us that day, and tentatively picked up my fork and tasted the food. Yes, it was good, but then everything that God does is good.

A miracle, by one definition, is something that does not occur everyday in the natural course of events. I think that this episode is perfectly qualified to be included in this category.

To fly or not to fly?

Is everything in life just a gamble, or is there a greater power at work invisible to human eyes?
Must we just leave everything to chance and live our lives as a lottery, hoping that we might see some good in our time?
I firmly believe that since I became a believer everything that I go through or encounter is within the scope of providence. What I mean by that is if God is truly God, and if He has an

interest in me, then I can totally trust Him with my life and my future. All that happens to me, all that is planned for me, is within His all-knowing foreknowledge.

Of course, such a trust can only be built on a real and very personal relationship with the Creator of this world. That relationship can only come about when I turn to Jesus and give my life over to Him. He said categorically, "I am the Way, I am the Truth, and I am the Life. No one comes to God the Father except through Me!"
Pretty tough words, but I have proved the truth of them time and time again.

To illustrate this I offer the following real-life example:

Towards the end of 1982 I was invited to address the National Conference in Lagos, Nigeria. There would be around seven thousand delegates, and I would be expected to speak once or twice every day for at least one week.

The advertising was under way in the Capital, and my picture was being posted out to the delegates. I would be away from home for the Christmas season which certainly was not my idea of fun, especially as it would be our baby's first Christmas. However, I settled myself, and packed my things in anticipation.

I would be travelling with a good friend of mine from Nigeria by the name of Jimmi Oshin. He had worked with me for several years here in the UK, and was desperate to get me out there to meet the various leaders.
I had had all of my 'jabs', and stocked up with anti-malaria and water-purifying tablets.

A week before we were due to fly, my ticket and visa had failed to materialise despite having made numerous telephone calls and visits to the High Commission in London. We were both getting a little concerned because of the arrangements and the schedule of the programme, and I began to wonder if God really wanted me to go. I knew that He was absolutely in control, and so made a suggestion to Him when I was praying on the Monday of that week.

I said, "OK, God, You know what is going on here, and I trust you with the situation."

I made a proposal, if you like, and said, "If the visa and ticket comes on Tuesday, Wednesday, or Friday, I will still fly out; but if they come on Thursday I will not go, and I will accept that as being your will and plan for me!"

Well, guess what! That visa and ticket came on Thursday!

My friend Jimmi telephoned me to congratulate me on their arrival, and asked me to meet him at the airport.

He was extremely annoyed when I declined. I told him the conditions that I had put on the matter, and said that I believed God had clearly shown me His decision regarding travelling. He became quite agitated, and hung up.

I did not speak to Jimmi again for about one month until after he returned from Lagos.

Well, wasn't I surprised when he informed me that on the day that he flew out there was a

military coup in Nigeria, and as a result, a curfew was placed on the capital?
Jimmi was locked inside the airport at Lagos for three weeks!

I, on the other hand, completely enjoyed Christmas at home with my family!

Miracles happen when you begin to place your absolute trust and faith in God.
As I have said before, such faith can only be born out of a living experience and spiritual encounter with Jesus Christ his Son!

Like the moon, when it comes into the right position, the miracle happens!

Walking on Water!

We've all heard the saying "walking on water", but it is not until you actually step out of the boat that you appreciate what it really means.

It is when you dare to do something that your mind argues is quite impossible! Most of us are rational beings who measure most of what we do with a deal of caution. What happens though, when you are called to put your whole life 'out on a limb'?

What if that calling comes simply from the notion that you believe God has spoken to you to do something? (Now, I should just point out that God will never tell us to do anything that is wrong or against the truth.)

You can not see Him, nevertheless you believe in your heart that He really is God, and that He does not make mistakes. You take on complete trust that He is equally concerned about your physical needs as He is your spiritual requirements.

You place your faith in an ancient book called the Bible, believing that God actually talks to you through its pages. You rest your life on that Book, and accept it to be holy, inspired, absolute truth, and authoritative; this is indeed the infallible word from God.

You believe that He plays an intimate role in your life, guiding you in every important decision that you will ever have to make.

That is not to say that every decision you ever make is the correct one (I've made some awful ones!), but if you give time and place for God to get in on the situation, He can and will reveal His plan and purpose for your life.

In the Bible, Peter was called to get out of a small fishing boat in the middle of a tempestuous sea, in the dark of the night, by a figure who appeared to be walking on top of the waves! The other guys in the ship must have thought him totally crazy! Can you just imagine the scene?

"Hey, Peter, don't be daft! What do you think you're doing? You'll die if you go out there!"

"Pete, have you been drinking, man?"

Now Peter was by no means stupid, but he had heard a compelling voice calling out through the wind and rain, "Come!"

Faith rose up in his heart, (he knew it was Jesus), and he said, "OK, I'm on my way!"

He climbed out of the boat, and placed his feet on the water.

If you hear God speak to you, you've really got to do something about it. You can't just sit there and do nothing. Oh yes, sure everyone else will tell you that you are going 'over the top' with your belief. They will suggest that you are being 'fanatical', and that you need to come down to earth. Even your very best friend will tell you to think it over before you do anything.

But when you know that it is God talking to you, you have got to step out, and trust Him with whatever happens!

I have done this on many occasions, and He has never failed me.

Let me give an example:

Perfect Timing!

It was the month of June 1989, and we had been living in the South West for some four years holding Gospel concerts around the country, and recording some of our work in the studio behind the house.

I heard that Dr. Billy Graham was in London for a few days conducting a mission in the East End at Upton Park Football Ground.

I suggested to my wife that we drive up to hear him and take a chance that we get a ticket for the evening's programme. So, taking our two children, we drove the five hours up to West Ham Stadium.

On our arrival at four in the afternoon, I was quite dismayed to learn from the stewards that all the tickets were gone, and that there was no chance of getting into the grounds without one.
I had truly believed that it was alright with God to go, and that He indeed wanted us to be there.

I walked away from the ticket office a wee bit flummoxed. I had not gone more than fifteen yards when I heard someone calling to me from the entrance to the stadium. I turned and walked back to the official who was beckoning to me, and he said that he had overheard me saying that I had driven up from Devon. He asked me whether I knew a certain gentleman by the name of Gordon Friend.

I was absolutely flabbergasted! I mean, Devon is some huge place! I said, "Do you mean the Gordon Friend of Overweir Farm?"

He said , "Yes, that's right!"

I told him that he was the treasurer in my home church, and I knew him very well! He said that I was not to worry about getting into the meeting as he would give us front-row seats, and furthermore, we could park our car in the stadium car park, reserved only for officials!

It was June the 16th, (a date that would become most significant), and I stood at the end of that evening on West Ham's 'sacred' turf, looking up into the dark sky through the blaze of hundreds of floodlights.

Thousands of people stood all around me, some were counsellors, and others what you might call 'seekers'. They were out there because of the message that Billy had just preached, and wanted to do some business with God.

I just felt that I wanted to be alone with God to hear what he wanted me to do with the rest of my life.

I guess that I must have been stood there for three quarters of an hour. I was absolutely convinced that God had shown me during that time that we were to leave Devon and do a new thing elsewhere in the country.

When I met up with my wife shortly after, I was not really surprised when she told me that she felt God wanted us to move from our house and go do something for Him!

Back in Devon we did not really know what the next step should be, but being convinced that God had told us it was time to leave the area we put the house on the market. I was invited, (through a series of those so-called 'coincidences'), to apply to work within a Christian organisation as the Pastor of a church. I had never done this before, and did not really think that it was quite my area of expertise. However, I filled in the forms and applied for a position within the denomination.

The process of application for the ministry is quite long and involved, and culminated in a three hour interview, or should I call it 'interrogation'?

We were to wait to find out if we were accepted. That was long, painful, and hard, especially as we had a buyer for the house in spite of the 'crash' in property prices at that time. (It was not our house, but as it belonged to a family trust, we had to put it on the market before moving).

We believed that we should move to Holyhead, off Anglesey in North Wales. We felt quite convinced that this was where God wanted us to be. We had travelled up there a couple of times that year, and each time we were there the impression was the same!

We felt a sense of destiny about the place.

I believe that God was telling us that we would go there to do something for Him!

It was the first of May 1990 when there was a knock at the door. I opened it to find the prospective buyer for our home in a rather agitated mood.

She explained that due to her and her husband being college lecturers, they really needed a date for moving in, - the sooner the better. I did not know what to say because we had not heard anything from our interview as to where or even if we might be stationed, but I knew that God was in perfect control of the whole thing. I felt that things were running a little ahead of schedule perhaps, but knew that I had to act in faith and commit myself to a decision right there and then.

I invited the lady in, and asked my wife to fetch a calendar. Kneeling on the lounge carpet, I sent a 'thought-prayer' out to God, and asked him to guide me with choosing a date for moving! You must remember that we had nowhere to move to at that moment in time!

My eyes fell upon the date Friday the 31st of May.

I had a sense of *'knowing'* that that was the date.

I told the woman that we would move out on that day and she could move in on Saturday the 1st June. She was delighted and left to inform her solicitor, whilst we telephoned ours to confirm the same.

I had a tremendous peace about it, and even when my wife said that I had now made us homeless, I knew that I could rely on God for the future. You see, I had learnt to spend a bit of time with God getting to know Him over the years, and as a result, I knew that I could trust him. He promised that He would never fail me or let me down, and He was not going to begin to do so now!

I said, "I know that we seem to be two weeks ahead of the situation, but we must act in faith. Who knows? Maybe we will get invited up to Holyhead on Friday the 31st and get an interview for the church on the Saturday!"

That evening at around 8 o'clock the telephone rang. A Scotsman on the other end introduced himself as an Elder from the Holyhead Church, and told me that he had just received a phone-call out of the blue from his Area Superintendent asking him to give me a call. It was suggested that the church interview us for the position of Minister!

Would we "come up on Friday 31st May, stay over, and have an interview on Saturday the 1st June?"

I slept very well that night!

Leaving all!

So, burning the bridges behind us, we moved up to Holyhead on May 31st, arriving on the Island of Anglesey at around 11pm. This was to avoid anyone seeing the removals van. We did not wish for anybody to know that we had actually moved, thus making ourselves homeless (effectively), and prejudicing the interview on Saturday. We hid the removals truck out of sight.

It was vital that the committee interviewing us did not feel obliged to take us on simply because we were landed on them.

We were asked some rather awkward questions during our two-hour meeting the following day, and had to tactfully avoid answering certain questions such as, "Do you have a 'vision' for Holyhead?", and, "When would you be able to move up?" I suggested that everyone on the committee needed to know for themselves from God whether we should be there or not.

It was a pleasant interview, but no decision was going to be made there and then, and we were told in those infamous words, "Thank you for coming. We'll let you know in due course."

The short journey back into the town was insufficient to deal with the big question-mark that hung in the air. How long would *We'll let you know in due course"* be?

We were homeless, with three little children, stranded in a place that was quite foreign to us, and none of the committee had the slightest inkling of our predicament.

But we had heard from God, and He would not let us down.

We had put all of our trust and faith in Him, and the problem was His, and not ours.

This is the assurance that you have when you belong to Christ.

We were staying in a large house that overlooked the Irish sea with a lovely family who were members of the same church. On arriving back there, we had barely sat down when there was a telephone call for us.

It was the Chairman of the Committee on the other end. He told us that for the first time in the history of the church the members had been unanimous in their decision!

Would we consider taking the job?

I said, "Yes".

He then asked when we would be able to move up to Anglesey!

I told him that we already had.

He was, in colloquial language, 'gob-smacked'!

About twenty minutes later we received another telephone call from a man calling himself David. He informed us that he was the Regional Superintendent, and wished to confirm our 'induction' (the actual starting date of our appointment, which would be characterised by an official service in the church).

This was to take place on the 16th June 1990 - exactly one year to the very hour when I first sensed God speaking to me on West Ham's turf! He said that he had something new for us to do, and here was the precise timing of His word.

We moved into a Church Pension Fund house the very next day!

When you step into the position of trusting God, miracles begin to flow!

The Winning Combination!

I had a dream one day, well, actually it was more than a dream. Ever since 1976 I have cherished a hope. A hope that I might actually be able to do something to change my country in some way!
What do I mean by that?
The last twenty years have seen our nation 'go to the dogs' both morally and spiritually.

A long time ago a gentleman by the name of Victor White said something to me that I will never forget. He was a member of the cult 'The Jehovah's Witnesses', and I enjoyed winding him up during lunch break at ITT's factory in St. Leonards, Sussex. He took me aside after one such occasion and said, "John, you are going to be a leader of others some day. You will either lead them into evil, or you will lead them into good. I hope that it will be the latter, but I'm afraid that it will probably be into evil."

As it turns out, I have become a leader of others, and over the past years I trust that I have led many into good and not into evil.

I love my country, and feel a great sense of loyalty and duty to it and its people. I know that there is a whole lot of talk these days about the British needing to find their 'identity', but I do not think that we have ever really lost it. This was never so profoundly obvious than when Princess Diana died in that tragic road accident in August 1997. The national shock that rocked Great Britain that awful morning rediscovered that identity like nothing else ever could.

We were a people in mourning.

Although the whole world shared our grief, it was *our* Princess that had died, and it was *we as a people* that suffered together both privately and publicly.

I, like so many others, felt drawn to London, to both Buckingham Palace and Kensington Palace. I felt a real sense of 'belonging' to these tens of thousands of people that converged on the Capital during that week.

I travelled down with my family on the Sunday following her funeral, and walked amongst the crowds outside Kensington Palace. You have to have actually been there to really grasp the depth of emotion and solemnity that literally hung in the air that night. Acres of bouquets blanketed the ground.

It must have been the day that the world ran out of flowers.

Three feet deep in many places, their fragrance drifted hundreds of yards across St. James's Park on that late summer's evening. As we walked amongst the people and just stood gazing at the awesome sight, my youngest son of seven years said, "Dad, this place is bad!" I said, "What do you mean?" He replied, "People shouldn't be talking here; its very sad." He, like my other two children, was very moved, and I was glad that they all had the privilege to be there and share in something quite profound.

Over the last ten years or so, we have seen some staggering tragedies in our nation.

There was of course the 1987 Stock Market collapse, when billions of pounds were wiped off share prices, and thousands of people lost their life-savings and investments. Interest rates soared, and the property market crashed through the floor.

Then there was Lockerbie. I remember sitting in front of the television watching the news reports, trying to come to terms with such premeditated violence. Seeing the bulkhead of that huge Pan-Am airliner lying in the field amongst bomb-blasted debris and dismembered bodies defied belief. The little child's doll lying in the mud, blackened by the explosion, declared the moral and spiritual bankruptcy of the perpetrators of such a crime. It was just before Christmas, and we felt so awful wrapping the presents that year for our children and friends.

Is this really the world I live in?

In that same twelve months there was the Clapham rail disaster in which so many people lost their lives.

My neighbour died the same night as the accident, and I remember his wife calling at my house the following morning to tell me that her husband had passed away. I was polite, and said, "I'm so sorry", but my heart was all taken up with the loss of the lives on the train. He was over eighty years old and had lived his life how he pleased. Careless of what he had been taught as a child in Sunday

School, and utterly disinterested in God, he went to a hopeless eternity. The only thing awaiting him would be the certainty of a judgement day when he, like every other, will be called before God to give account.

Some of the victims in the disaster were just young people with their whole lives before them, suddenly cut short, and taken away. Perhaps they had never heard the wonderful truth of God's love for this world of sinners.

March 13th 1996, and things got worse. Sixteen precious little children and their devoted teacher were shot dead in cold blood in Dunblane, Scotland. Many of us cried and held our children closer as we collected them from school.

How could this be?

What is it going to take to bring this nation to its senses and bend it back toward God? What sort of 'shock' is needed to cause a people like us to repent, and turn again to the truth?

I said that I love my country, but that does not mean that I love it as it is or how it is run. In fact, for a nation that has such a grand Christian heritage, it is in a terrible condition.

Change of government does not change people, but *changed* people can alter a nation's destiny.

I was walking down to the beach one morning about four years ago when I had the most strong impression that I must do something to touch the nation. Something that would somehow challenge the 'staus quo'.

I believe God was speaking to me. I had grown used to this form of inspiration. I laughed to myself, and thought, "Who me? Who am I to think that I could do anything?"

But the message was reiterated, and I was left with a strong sense that this really was God, and if He had suggested it, then He could also supply all that it would take to accomplish the same.

It was some months later that I was in a video editing suite near Manchester, when somebody said, "You know, John, you could make a ten minute video with a short, sharp, message on it, and retail it for 99p! At that price you could get thousands out around the country."

That was it!

I telephoned Rank Videos in London and asked to meet with a representative. Was it really possible to achieve this, and get the greatest news in all the world onto a ten minute video?

I met with Paul (from Rank) at a Little Chef on the M6 in Cheshire. After describing what it was I wanted to do, he asked me to explain my faith to him. How was it possible to believe in someone you could not see? How does such a faith work?

I told him the story of Blondin, the famous tightrope walker and acrobatist who stretched a wire right across the Niagara Falls from Canada to America. He then proceeded to walk across that wire with a long balancing pole. Then he went over the thundering waters with nothing in his hands at all. A bit later he took a wheelbarrow over on that thin wire, and then returned with it loaded with potatoes! He was applauded in both countries, and a host of reporters pressed on him to go again. The crowds loved it, and voiced their admiration. He turned to the crowd and said, "Do you believe that I could put a man in this wheelbarrow and take him across safely?" One rather loudmouthed fellow near to him (so it is reported) said, "Yes, Yes, I believe that you can do it!" Blondin replied, "OK, jump in!" Well, I guess that chap wished that he had never opened his mouth, and slunk back into the crowd!

I explained to Paul that this is what faith is all about. It is trusting your life to somebody else, - to somebody bigger than you.

After working out the costings and double-checking all my figures, it actually appeared quite possible to make the film and be able to sell it for just 99p!

There were two reasons that I felt ninety nine pence was the right price. The first was simply that anybody could afford to give away the video at that amount, and this was very important because the film was to contain the most important message that anyone could ever hear.

The second reason was based on a story in the Bible. It was about a farmer who had 100 sheep, but had lost one. His love and concern for that one runaway was so great that he left the ninety nine sheep in the care of his farm-hands, and went out all night into the storm and rain over the precarious countryside looking for it.
He did not return until he had found it in all of its misery and loneliness, and, putting it on his shoulder, wounded and cold, returned to his home. When he got back, he called all of his friends and neighbours round for a celebration supper, and said, "Rejoice and celebrate with me, because I have found my sheep that was lost!"

The conclusion or moral of the story that Jesus told here was that there is ecstatic joy and happiness in heaven when one sinner returns to God!
In fact, God has more delight and pleasure when just one sinner turns to Him, than when all the

Christians in the country have a great get-together in Wembley Stadium!

The 99p price-tag represents the ninety nine sheep that were safe in the barn, and the video, being given out, reaches the one who is lost and far away, to bring them into the safety of the fold.

But on with my story.........

I knew that it was going to take many thousands of pounds to produce the film, and many more thousands to purchase the first twenty thousand videos from Rank.

On top of that I wanted to produce a good quality booklet to send free of charge to anyone who felt inspired by the contents of the video. I intended to print forty thousand copies of this full-colour brochure to begin! I had absolutely no salary or income, having resigned my position with the church some months earlier.

While I was out walking across the fields one morning, and just sort of talking to God about the finances of such an operation, I felt that He wanted me to take a new step forward in the programme.

I was to do something that I had never done before. I was to book a conference lounge in a Post House hotel on the M6 near Birmingham, and then telephone Lawrence, who I had met just a few weeks previously, to ask for his assistance. He was a tall, middle-aged man who never quite knew when to stop talking! His job was to find me forty people who might be interested in my vision, who would be willing to come to the hotel for a buffet and presentation on Friday 27th January 1995.

I could not really afford the hotel, let alone a hot buffet, but I just went for it in faith!

It snowed that week, and the roads were pretty awful on the Friday, but the motorway at least was clear. I set off early to set up the head-table in the hotel ready for the evening.

To my disappointment just twelve people turned up, six of them being my personal friends, who themselves probably could not even have afforded to contribute towards the meal!

We had the buffet first, which was certainly worth coming out for on that freezing cold night!

I then proceeded to share my heart about my concern for the moral and spiritual state of our country.

I spoke of the need to communicate with people in a realistic way, outlining the concept of the video.

I felt that it was well received, and concluded the evening with a cup of coffee and a prayer. At no time did I ask for money or donations, yet before we left, there were enough gifts in cash and cheques to pay in full for the hotel and the meal.

One chap who came sat two chairs along from me, well actually, he slumped in his chair and leaned heavily on the table. I wondered why he had come really, and who had invited him! He went back to the buffet three times, and for most of the evening appeared quite uninterested in what I was saying. Although he managed a couple of questions during the question-time, I figured that someone had made a mistake in having him there!

Having said that, I believed that the event had been worthwhile, and I knew that God was always in control, and sensed His peace on my life.

About one week later there was a knock at my front door. There on my doorstep was this very same chap dressed in his work-clothes. He asked if I remembered him. I most certainly did! It was his lunch-break, and he wondered if I might have a few minutes to chat.

We had a cup of cafetiere coffee, and he told me, much to my astonishment, that he really enjoyed the presentation. He said that he believed that it was truly from God, and would like to be of some help if he could.

He suggested that he might have £300 saved up under his pillow for a rainy day, and asked whether it would be of any use to us. I said, "Yes please, *anything* would help at the moment!"

He had to get back to work, but promised that he would call again the following week for a coffee.

He did come back, and we did have another coffee, or two! We chatted about the video and its production and the possibilities of reaching our nation with its message, and then it was time for him to go back to work.

Just as he was leaving he handed me a crumpled white envelope. He told me that it was the £300 he had mentioned before, and said that he knew that God wanted him to give it to me. I took it and said "Thank you", and being typically English, did not open it until he had driven off!

Pulling the cheque from the envelope, I stared in amazement and wonder at its value. There, in the right-hand box, was the amount - £19,500-00! Yes, even in the scribbled writing it said, *Nineteen Thousand and Five Hundred pounds!*

Isn't God incredible?

And that is how the Winning Combination was birthed!

We have seen so many miracles in the financial area that it would take several large chapters to record them all. Each of them was in direct answer to a specific prayer, -

and people say that God is not real!!

The Bible says that it is the fool who says to himself, "There is no God"!

On one occasion just this year we really needed £5,000 for the work, in a hurry. I went out for my walk with God in the morning and just mentioned it to Him. He's my friend, you see, so I don't get too embarrassed talking these things over with Him.

Three days later a lady walked into our operations base and handed me the answer. Inside the letter was a cheque for six thousand pounds! She told me that God had told her to give it.

God is able to do exceedingly more than we ever dare think or ask of Him!

You might well ask how I know when God is talking with me. It is somewhat hard to explain, but you have to have this *'faith'* thing before you can ever really understand.

There was this man called 'Nico' who really wanted to know about having faith, who recognised that the miracles that Jesus performed came from God, but could not figure it all out. He was himself a very religious man, but had no personal experience or relationship with God. (You can read all about it in the Bible in John chapter 3).

He came to Jesus one night to try and find the answer, and Jesus turned to him and said, "Nico, unless you are 'born again' you can not *see* or even begin to *understand* the kingdom of God".

"Well", said he, somewhat astonished, "How can a man be born when he is old? Can he get back inside his mother and be re-born?"

Jesus explained that he needed a *'spiritual'* rebirth before he could ever understand about faith, or talking to God, or having a personal relationship with Him.

He said that just like a person is born physically, so he or she must be born *'spiritually'* . This is essential if ever they are to understand the mysteries and secrets of God's kingdom.

He went on to compare the spiritual life to the wind. He said, "The wind blows wherever it choses, and you can hear the sound of it (you can see its effect), but you can not tell where it came from or where it will go next. This is what it is like with every person who is 'born-again'."

You see, when anybody turns to God in *faith*, and *accepts* the truth about Jesus Christ, they become a new person (a new creation). The Bible says that old things pass away, and all things become new! God sends His Holy Spirit into their heart and gives them a *spiritual* dimension. This gives them a unique and personal relationship with their

Creator, and results in a wonderful *knowing* of God.

And it is all because God so loved (and still loves) the world that He gave His only Son Jesus Christ, so that whoever believes in Him (hands over their life to Him) shall not perish, but have everlasting life.

He did not send His Son into the world to condemn it and judge it, but He sent Him to save it!

(There is coming a day soon, however, when He will indeed come to judge it, and bring it to its final end.)

The greatest Miracle of all.

This happened to me many years ago. I was in the East End of London in a small flat in High Street North, living my life how I pleased. My ambitions were to make loads of money, marry a gorgeous girl, live life to the full, and stay alive as long as I could.

All of those things were uncertain at the best of times, and I ended up working for the London Co-op!

Then one day I got to thinking about what would happen if I were to die. I know that it is not the sort of thing a young man should be thinking about, but why not? Death does not affect only the old.

I figured that I would never make heaven, (God being so holy, and me, - well....!) and that left only hell as an alternative. This thought occupied my mind for some days, and, returning from work one evening, I knelt down on the carpet in my sparsely furnished living room, and tried praying. I had heard the 'gospel' when I was a child, and knew that Jesus had died on a cross for sinners. I easily came into that category, so I just told Him what was in my heart. If He was truly God, then He already knew all about me anyway, and everything that I had ever said and done.

It felt as though He were in the same room as me, and I thought that I could almost reach out and touch Him! Although I knew that He had risen from the dead and was very much alive, I seemed to see Him hanging on a dirty, rough, cross under a darkened sky. It looked as though it were the middle of the night, and as if the burdens of the whole world were crushing down on Him.

He looked right into my eyes, piercing my very soul, and said, "*You* are the cause of My pain! *You* are the reason for this sacrifice!"

"And I love you!"

"And I forgive you!"

"And here on this cross I pay the price, in full, for your life, and the right to your heart!"

I asked Him to forgive my many sins and to clean out my life. I asked Him to come into my heart and give me a new start.

He did.

I just knew that He had. I felt clean, forgiven, healthy, and brand new!

I heard no audible voice, neither did I see any flashes of lightning, but I knew beyond any doubt that He had done something in me that was going to revolutionise my life forever!

He was *real* all of a sudden, not just some great Being up there in the sky somewhere. He was with me, and I knew that He would never let me go.

I said, "Jesus, if you are going to take me on, then you must take me lock, stock, and barrel!" That meant that everything I was, the situation I was in, my past, my present, my future, were all His responsibility.

I got me a Bible and started to read the Gospel of John. Suddenly that old Book started to make some incredible sense. It was alive, and God began to speak to me through the words that were on those pages!

I had to sort out some things in my life which I knew were wrong, and that surprised a few people, I can tell you!

I told my family and some friends what had happened to me. They were astonished, and agreed that something had indeed been done.

That was over twenty years ago, and by virtue of that change of position in my life, I have enjoyed a wonderful friendship with God ever since.

You can too.

The same Christ looks down at you right now, and says, *"I love you, I forgive you, no matter how bad you've been; no matter how messed up your life is; I will receive you as My son, My daughter, and give you a brand new start!"*

You may be a 'backslider' who once knew God in a real way, but like the prodigal, you've gone your own way. You've wrecked your life, you've spoiled your chances, - but God is willing to receive you back the very moment you step toward him in faith.

He still loves you! I promise you - He does!

He brings hope for your future - He has a plan for your life.

A Broken Plant -
A Wrecked Life!

A flash of white over in the grass caught my attention whilst out walking one morning. I have always had a keen interest in the countryside since a child. Every Sunday my father would take us (my sisters and I) for a walk in the country down Rock Lane to 'Three Oaks'. There, during the Spring and Summer, we would be rewarded for every new wild flower that we could find growing in the hedgerows. Threepence most times, but if the plant was a rare one, we might get a silver sixpence!

Even now, it still amazes me just how beautiful and varied the English countryside is, and I still find myself looking out for that new undiscovered rarity.

This particular morning just a few weeks ago, my mind was having half-an-hour off before the day began in earnest.

Attracted by this splash of colour in the grass, I walked over to what turned out to be a type of multi-headed daisy that grew to about three feet tall. Unfortunately this particular flower appeared to have been trodden down by some cruel boot at some time, and rather than standing erect and tall, it lay along the ground, crippled, damaged, and broken.

Yet, in spite of its handicap and deformity, it had turned its whole head skyward, and, looking up into the radiance of the sun, displayed a beauty and glory that shouted out, "Hey! look at me!"

I had a 'Wobbly-Man' when I was very little. This was a plastic toy in the shape of a clown, but instead of feet it had a rounded bottom that was weighted. This meant that no matter what you did to Mr. Wobbly, he would always end up the right way up!

You could kick him, throw him against the wall, drop him, roll him, slap him, but no matter what you did to try and put one over on him, he always, but always, came back up smiling! I think of myself sometimes as that Mr. Wobbly!

As I looked on this damaged flower it reminded me of my own life in some peculiar way. This plant was supposed to be upright and perfect in all its ways. It should be standing proud giving testimony to its Creator as that of a wonderful designer, a caring benefactor, and a loving friend.

And yet, in spite of its condition, - No! - I say because of its condition, it did all the more represent its Creator as a wonderful designer, a caring and kind benefactor, and a genuine friend!

I wish I could say that all my life has been upright and pure, that I have never 'messed up', that I have never been hurt or damaged, that there are no blemishes, but alas, that is not true.

I suppose that I have failed as much as any one else. Even as a Christian, I have 'blown it' on occasion and wrecked my life.

But here is the wonder! - out of the mess, the failure, the broken ruins, the light still shines! Just like that flower, though broken and smashed, yet somehow, by God's mercy, love, and goodness, and a rather special miracle, this flower turns its face toward heaven above and declares the truth that "God is love"!

When I have found myself in the lowest valley, the darkest night of my life, I have turned myself back towards God. By His goodness and love, He has restored me, forgiven me, healed me, and shined His light into my life. Just like Psalm 23 in the Bible says, "He restores my soul" He picks me up again.

There's a whole lot of us people out there who are well wrecked. We've been told that we are rubbish, failures, useless, unwanted and unnecessary! A waste of space! We could have been so good, so useful, so full of potential!

But God is bigger than all of us, and there is nothing impossible to Him!

I went back over there just this week and looked for that flower.
Somebody had ripped it out and discarded it on the rubbish tip.

Thank you God, that you don't!

I've got a special Friend who I run to when I'm in trouble. He never refuses to hear me out, nor stands in judgement over me. Even when I know that I am desperately wrong, and when He knows the same, he doesn't stand there saying, "I told you so!" "You made your bed, - you lie on it!"
He has compassion even in the worst scenario, and seeks for a way to restore, rebuild, and mend the damaged goods of my life.

When you were just a child (if you were anything like me) it seemed like you got hit every time that you did something wrong. The only possible value in such action was that of a threatening nature. You didn't do it again because you didn't want to get the stick!

In fact, it just made you more careful in the way you behaved in the future simply to avoid getting found out! There was often no mercy (that you could see) in such punishments, but of course you were politely told that, *"this is going to hurt me more than it hurts you!"* Oh yea?

My special Friend is always consistent. Perhaps that is why I wrote this little verse one day,

When no-one knows, He knows;
When no-one cares, He cares;
When no-one loves, He keeps on loving,
That's why I know that I can trust Him!

I remember Him telling me something most profound, and something that has been of great power and effect in my life over the last fifteen years. I was driving through the beautiful countryside of North Wales at the time, and journeyed through a wonderful mountain range.

The little road that I was travelling on wound its way along the side of those majestic mountains, and I felt constrained to stop the jeep and walk over to the side of the track. Something had caught my eye!

Looking across the valley to the huge mountain rising up into the skies, I noticed what looked like hundreds of little white veins running haphazardly from the top and all the way down its sides. Leaning against the railings I peered down from the road into the valley below. At the bottom there was the most wonderful picture of tranquillity that one might hope to find anywhere. A perfectly still lake stretched itself out in the blazing sunshine, and I could make out the splendour of a glorious pine forest to one end with a lush green blanket of grass running down to the water's edge.

It quickly became clear that the white zig-zagging streaks on the mountain were in fact little streamlets coursing their way down the terrain: crystal clear water forever seeking a path down into the basin below, and increasing both in quantity and power the further it went, until finally, it crashed into the lake as a mighty torrent.

I really sensed my Friend speaking to me. He said, "John, you see all this?" I nodded my head. "This is just like my love towards you. Those streams are a picture of My love. It doesn't matter how low the valley you may find yourself in at times; it doesn't matter how deep the pit you may have fallen into; just as water always seeks the lowest level, so My love will ever seek you, even at the very lowest situation in your life!"

"There is no valley so deep that My love cannot reach you!"

Now, I have been in some low places. Sometimes through no fault of my own, and sometimes because of my own folly and waywardness, but even in the darkest night and the most lonely of circumstances, God's love has reached down to me and picked me up! My Friend has kept His word and found a way to get a hold of me. The deeper the valley, the more powerful His love and mercy appears!

You may be in dire straits at this very moment; maybe your whole world is crumbling all around you. Pressures and difficulties, financial impossibilities, wrecked relationships, broken families, poor health - I don't know your particular situation, but let me recommend my Friend. His name is Jesus, and He has promised to anyone who is worn-out, under pressure, at the very point of giving up, to come to Him, to call on His name in faith, and He will rescue them and save them out of their troubles.

"Come unto Me all of you who are weary, sad and burdened with a heavy load, and I will give you rest - rest to your soul!"

"Call on Me in the day of trouble, and I will deliver you, and you will give me thanks!"

He can deliver your miracle the very moment that you stand in the position of faith, trust, and confidence.

So, how do I get this faith?

Well, actually, it is quite simple, and maybe that is what makes it so difficult for people to grasp!

Faith is a *gift* from God.

You can not have faith by *trying* to have faith! To be precise, it comes by hearing. As you have read this book, so you have heard truths about God. The Bible says that faith comes by hearing, and hearing comes by the word of God. (That is why you should read the Bible).

If somehow God has spoken to you through these pages, then faith will have begun to rise in your heart.

I can not make anyone believe in God, or in the truth about Jesus. I am just like that moon that hangs there in the darkness. I have no light or power or life of my own, but all that I can do is reflect (in some very small way) the truth of God's love to this degenerate world.

God is the light, and only He can shine into your darkness and bring life, and joy, and hope, and peace.

Jesus said, "I am the light of this world; if any one follows Me, they shall not walk in darkness, but have the light of life!"

The greatest miracle that could happen to you right now is that you believe with all of your heart in Jesus Christ. And to do that you must do three things. You must firstly believe that He is the True Son of God, that He died for you on the cross in order that you might be forgiven and washed from all of your sin by His blood.

Secondly, you must be willing to repent. That is an old fashioned word, but so relevant today. What it simply means is that you must 'about-turn'. Turn from the direction that you are going in, and turn to God. Turn from what you know is wrong or evil, or sinful, and face Jesus Christ as the only one who can save you.

And thirdly, you must receive this Jesus into your heart and accept His *free* gift of salvation. The Bible says that whoever receives Jesus Christ and accepts Him as their only Saviour, becomes a child of God. You cannot earn this or buy it. God's forgiveness, love, and salvation, is totally free to whoever will receive it!

To receive Jesus into your life you could pray this simple prayer:

Oh God, I acknowledge that I am a sinner. Please forgive my sin. Wash me with the blood that Jesus shed at the cross, and make me clean. I believe on Jesus with all my heart and ask Him to come into my heart right now. Fill me with Your Holy Spirit, and make me Your child. I ask it in the name of Your holy Son Jesus, Amen.

Better still, tell Him the truth of where you are, of what you have been, and that you need Him right now to become your friend and Master (we call Him Lord). Talk to Him as the One who knows everything there is to know about you. He has watched you since the day that you were born.

And now, if you have prayed that prayer, you should tell somebody. Don't keep it to yourself! God says that if you believe you will not be ashamed to confess your personal faith in Jesus Christ. Get a Bible and begin to read the New

Testament, and pray - it is not hard! Just talk to God as though He were your greatest friend - He is!

And it is so important to join a church or meet with other Christians friends who believe the same things about God and the Bible as are written in this book. There is an address at the back for you to write to, or telephone, or just go along to.

There is nothing too hard for God!

No, your life and circumstances are not too difficult for Him!

Whatever your need, however desperate your situation, God can perform a miracle for you the moment that you dare to step out and trust Him with all of your heart.

I have proved Him again and again. He has never failed me.

Why don't you just say, "Yes" to Him, and receive Him right now?

I shall leave you with the words of a song that I wrote some years ago to express my gratitude to God for all that He has done for me. I hope you like it.

I cannot understand , O, God,
How You could love someone like me;
I don't suppose I'll ever know why You should send Your
I do not know the reason why,   [Son;
I can't explain why He should die
And freely give away His life
For all that I have said and done.

And this one thing I'll never know
How God Himself could come below,
And humble Himself as just another mortal man;
And live amongst the people He made,
The very ones for whom He prayed
And said to them, "Come unto Me
Just as you are, you know you can!"

He healed the sick, and raised the dead;
He took the cripple from his bed;
He sat the little children right there upon His knee.
He touched the blind, and gave them sight,
He said, "I am this dark world's light;
My life I freely give for you,
So hear the truth, and be made free!"

And still I cannot understand
How You can love me as I am!
I'm not the sort of person that can help Your work along!
And heaven seems too good for me,
To live forever endlessly,
To be forgiven, and made Your child –
Oh surely Lord, You must be wrong?

I hear You give a brand-new start
To any with believing heart;
New life begins, and old things are passed away!
Indwelt by heavenly energy,
The future has a hope for me,
The night has gone, the light's come in,
The dawning of a brand-new day!

Oh God, reach out and take my hand,
And lift me up, and let me stand,
Make me the person You have wanted me to be!
Give me the faith that trusts in You,
Show me the work You'd have me do,
Transform my life, renew my heart,
Oh Jesus, live Your life in me!

Oh Lord, my words can never bring
Sufficient thanks, nor can I sing
A melody or song that shows my gratitude and love!
'Cos every time I close my eyes
And point my thoughts towards the skies
I hear the greatest love-song
Coming down to me from heaven above –

"For God so loved the world, He gave His only
Begotten Son, so that whoever believes on Him
should not perish, but have everlasting life!"

John chapter 3, verse 16 (the Bible)

This book comes with the compliments of: